Writing Letters

AGS

by
Mary Ellen Snodgrass

AGS®

American Guidance Service, Inc.
4201 Woodland Road
Circle Pines, MN 55014-1796
1-800-328-2560

Printed in the United States of America

ISBN 0–7854–0967–X (Previously ISBN 0–88671–963–1)

Product Number 90882

A 0 9 8 7 6 5 4

Contents

Introduction

These days people telephone their friends and family, send business mail by telegraph, TELEX, FAX machines, and e-mail (electronic mail), and use modems and computer networks, such as the World Wide Web, known as the Internet, to pass large amounts of information from one office complex to another or from one person to another. It may seem that letter writing is not very important. Yet nothing could be further from the truth.

Letters provide written and signed proof of one person's message to another. They can be filed, duplicated, reread, and offered as evidence of business transactions, promises made, and personal comments on a variety of matters. Moreover, handwritten letters symbolize a little piece of the sender's personality through the curve of letters, spacing of words, and style of presentation. All of these factors are as unique to the letter writer as eye color, tone of voice, or handshake.

Another important aspect of letters is their value to history. Telephone calls quickly pass away and leave no trace. Letters, on the other hand, remain behind as proof of at least one side of a relationship. Famous letters from the past tell of battles won or of friendships begun, as well as of the hopes and dreams of the writer. Like photographs, personal letters capture much of the writer's personality and feelings.

Proper letter-writing technique is a sign of good manners. It indicates that someone has taken the time and trouble to put words on paper and send them to another person. This effort proves sincere interest and concern for the receiver. When letter writing is combined with attractive stationery, ink, and stamps or a professional letterhead and an easily readable computer type style, the sender proves that communication with the receiver is a worthwhile, meaningful activity.

Friendly Letters

If you have family or friends who live in another part of town, in another city, or even in another country, you may want to write frequent, friendly letters. These letters follow a pattern. Friendly letters are

➤ informal and uncomplicated
➤ personal in tone (style or manner of expression in writing)
➤ generous with details and specifics
➤ usually written in longhand
➤ composed on cards, notepaper, or full-sized stationery

Like all letters, friendly letters need to follow some kind of form. They should tell something about what you are doing. They should also express your interest in the person who will receive them. Also they should answer any questions that the receiver may have asked in a previous letter.

Letters to Close Friends

The sample letter on page 7 shows the basic structure of the friendly letter, which includes the following parts.

➤ Heading

This section, written in the upper right-hand corner of the page, contains three lines. The first line provides the sender's street address. The second line names the city, state, and ZIP code. Since you are the sender, the address information on the first two lines will be your address. The third line lists the date on which the letter was written. For example:

> 7011 Lincoln Place
> Boston, Massachusetts 02111
> November 19, 1999

Note that in letters to very close friends or relatives, many people omit their address. However, the date is usually included.

➤ Greeting

The personal part of a friendly letter starts with the greeting. Skip a line after the date. Then begin this section at the far left-hand side of the page. It may open with any word that establishes friendly contact. For example:

> Hi Sam,
> Dear Aunt Ruth,
> Hello at last,
> Greetings from my new desk,
> My dear Rhoda,

Whatever friendly opening you choose, begin the greeting with a capital letter and end it with a comma. Within the greeting, capitalize only proper names and initials, as in Mrs. Jenkins, Cousin Dana, L. C., or Mother.

➤ Body

The most important part of the friendly letter is the body, in which you write a personal message. The message should contain specific questions about what you want to know about the person's activities, information about what you are doing, and answers to questions the person may have asked in a previous letter.

If you are telling about the activities of other people, quote some sentences just as they were spoken. Set off the part that is quoted by enclosing it in quotation marks. For example:

> Mark wants to know how you like mowing lawns. He said, "Jed never liked work that made him sweat!"

The body is made up of paragraphs. Each paragraph covers a different topic. To show that you are beginning a paragraph, indent the first line about five spaces or the width of your index finger.

➤ Closing

The closing shows that you are finished with your letter. It is placed below the body of the letter and aligns with the heading. There are many ways to close a friendly letter. Choose one that fits the tone of your message and the person to whom the letter is being sent. For example:

Always your friend,	(friendly)
With lots of love,	(affectionate)
See you soon,	(casual)
Your favorite nephew,	(loving)

Notice that the closing follows the same rules for capitalization and punctuation as the greeting.

➤ Signature

One of the key parts of a friendly letter is the signature. This section is your unique stamp, a proof that you composed this letter yourself. The signature is written right below the closing. Even if you type your letter or compose it on a word processor, your name is written out in longhand.

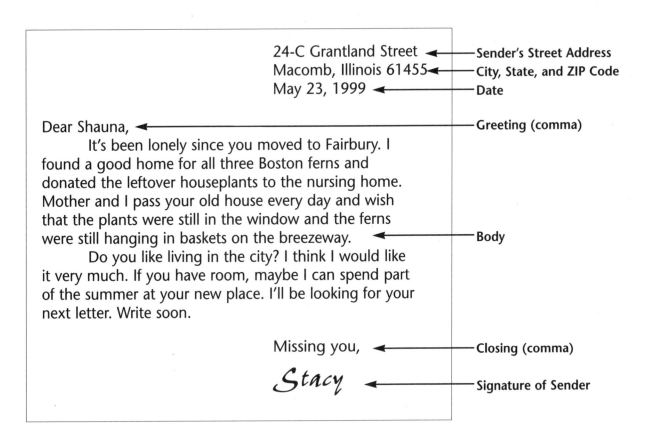

24-C Grantland Street ◄——— **Sender's Street Address**
Macomb, Illinois 61455◄——— **City, State, and ZIP Code**
May 23, 1999 ◄——— **Date**

Dear Shauna, ◄——————————————— **Greeting (comma)**
    It's been lonely since you moved to Fairbury. I found a good home for all three Boston ferns and donated the leftover houseplants to the nursing home. Mother and I pass your old house every day and wish that the plants were still in the window and the ferns were still hanging in baskets on the breezeway. ◄——— **Body**
    Do you like living in the city? I think I would like it very much. If you have room, maybe I can spend part of the summer at your new place. I'll be looking for your next letter. Write soon.

                Missing you, ◄——— **Closing (comma)**

                Stacy ◄——— **Signature of Sender**

After you have written a friendly letter, you should review the finished product to make sure that you have included everything. Answering the following list of questions is a good way to check yourself. Use the list to decide whether the letter on this page is written in proper form. Check for errors or omissions. Answer *Yes* or *No* to each statement.

_____ 1. Have I placed a heading in the top right-hand corner?

_____ 2. Is my mailing address on the top line?

_____ 3. Did I include the city, state, and five-digit ZIP code?

_____ 4. Do today's month, day, and year follow the address?

_____ 5. Did I skip a line before placing a greeting?

_____ 6. Is there a comma following the greeting?

_____ 7. Have I indented each paragraph five spaces?

_____ 8. Did I write about only one topic per paragraph?

_____ 9. Did I enclose direct quotations in quotation marks?

_____ 10. Have I placed the closing directly below the heading?

_____ 11. Did I put a comma after the closing?

_____ 12. Did I sign my name directly below the closing?

P.O. Box 1445
Charlotte, North Carolina

Dear Aunt Lydia

    I am coming to see you soon. Do you think that I might stay over the Fourth of July after my parents leave? I hope you say yes. Buddy wants me to tell you that he will be writing to you soon. He said, Tell Aunt Lydia that I am out of stamps. You know Buddy—always an excuse!

Love to all,
Ramona

Writing a letter is only part of the job. Each letter must be placed in an envelope. The receiver's address on the envelope must include enough accurate information so that the post office can deliver the letter. If the letter cannot be delivered, the sender's address must be included so that the letter can be returned.

Stacy Radcliffe
24-C Grantland St.
Macomb IL 61455

                        Ms. Shauna Mahaffey
                        Apt. 122-A Middleton Ave.
                        Fairbury IL 61739-2071

Notice some differences between the envelope and the original letter. The sender's address goes in the upper left-hand corner of the envelope. The sender's full name, often preceded by a title, comes before the street address, city, state, and five-digit ZIP code. The state's name is given in the two-letter postal code. The receiver's full name, street address, city, state, and ZIP code appear in the lower right-hand portion. The stamp goes in the upper right-hand corner. The names and addresses are printed or typed. Abbreviations may be used for the titles of people and for street names, such as *street, court,* or *avenue.* No periods or commas are used. A hyphen should appear between the five-digit ZIP code and the four-digit ZIP-plus-four number that may follow.

Postal Codes
The **postal code** is neither a full word nor an abbreviation. It is formed by two capital letters and is never followed by a period. It is a code created by the United States Post Office. Here are the postal codes for the 50 states and the District of Columbia.

AL	Alabama	MT	Montana
AK	Alaska	NE	Nebraska
AZ	Arizona	NV	Nevada
AR	Arkansas	NH	New Hampshire
CA	California	NJ	New Jersey
CO	Colorado	NM	New Mexico
CT	Connecticut	NY	New York
DC	District of Columbia	NC	North Carolina
DE	Delaware	ND	North Dakota
FL	Florida	OH	Ohio
GA	Georgia	OK	Oklahoma
HI	Hawaii	OR	Oregon
ID	Idaho	PA	Pennsylvania
IL	Illinois	RI	Rhode Island
IN	Indiana	SC	South Carolina
IA	Iowa	SD	South Dakota
LA	Louisiana	TN	Tennessee
KS	Kansas	TX	Texas
KY	Kentucky	UT	Utah
ME	Maine	VT	Vermont
MD	Maryland	VA	Virginia
MA	Massachusetts	WA	Washington
MI	Michigan	WV	West Virginia
MN	Minnesota	WI	Wisconsin
MS	Mississippi	WY	Wyoming
MO	Missouri		

Abbreviations

Often envelopes contain abbreviations, such as *Apt.,* the abbreviation for *apartment.* Many words connected with addresses are abbreviated so that the envelope is not overloaded with long, difficult words. For example:

Ave.	Avenue	Nat'l.	National
Bldg.	Building	Pk.	Park or Peak
Blvd.	Boulevard	P.O.	Post Office
Ct.	Court	Pres.	President
Ctr.	Center	Prov.	Province
Dr.	Doctor or Drive	Rd.	Road
Ft.	Fort	Rev.	Reverend
Hdqrs.	Headquarters	RFD	Rural Free Delivery
Jr.	Junior	Rte.	Route
Mr.	Mister	Sq.	Square
Mrs.	Indicates a married woman	St.	Street
Ms.	Indicates any woman	Terr.	Territory
Mt.	Mount or Mountain		

Folding Letters

The letter is usually folded horizontally into thirds and inserted into the envelope. If the writing paper is much wider than the envelope, the letter may be folded in half horizontally, and then folded in thirds.

folded in thirds

folded in half, then in thirds

A Match each of the following postal codes with the letter of the full name of the state. You will have answers left over when you finish.

_____ **1.** AK   _____ **5.** MA   _____ **9.** MS

_____ **2.** AL   _____ **6.** ME   _____ **10.** NE

_____ **3.** AR   _____ **7.** MD   _____ **11.** ND

_____ **4.** AZ   _____ **8.** MO   _____ **12.** NV

a. Nevada   **f.** North Dakota   **k.** Massachusetts

b. Missouri   **g.** North Carolina   **l.** Mississippi

c. Maryland   **h.** Maine   **m.** Montana

d. Arizona   **i.** Minnesota   **n.** Arkansas

e. Alaska   **j.** Alabama   **o.** Nebraska

B Write each of the following words in abbreviated form as you would write it on an envelope.

_____ **1.** National   _____ **6.** Fort

_____ **2.** Square   _____ **7.** President

_____ **3.** Avenue   _____ **8.** District of Columbia

_____ **4.** Boulevard   _____ **9.** Reverend

_____ **5.** Territory   _____ **10.** Rural Free Delivery

C Refer to the model letter on page 7 and the model envelope on page 9. Address the envelope below with both the sender's address and the receiver's address. Use both postal codes and ZIP codes to complete the address. As a final point, don't forget to draw in a stamp in the upper right-hand corner. Then fill out the form on page 13 with a response from Shauna to Stacy. Include information about Shauna's move to a new home and questions to Stacy about how things have changed since Shauna left. Divide your comments into paragraphs. Don't forget proper punctuation for the greeting and the closing.

_____

_____

_____

_____ ,

_____

_____

_____

_____

_____

_____

_____

_____

_____

_____

_____ ,

_____

Sometimes friendly communications take the form of a postcard, which usually displays a decorative picture on the front. It contains the following parts:

➤ The back of the postcard is divided by a vertical line into two halves.
➤ The left half contains a message, which must be carefully squeezed in to fit the small writing space.
➤ The right half contains the receiver's address.
➤ Postage goes at the top of the right-hand corner.

Notice that the postcard resembles a friendly letter in that it contains a communication to the receiver. The postcard differs from a friendly letter because there is no envelope and no space for the sender's address. If a postcard is improperly addressed, the post office will be unable to return it. Here is an example of the back of a decorative postcard:

Juan,

   Our bowling team finished first in the league! We split a check for $100. I hope we get to compete again this summer at a state tournament. The prize is a trip to Myrtle Beach. Wish us luck.

   See you later,

   Andy

Pvt Juan Muñoz
102 Whaler's Dr.
Anchorage AK 99526

Another type of postcard gives the sender more space to write. This is the postal card available from the post office. It is a handy form for entering contests, writing for tickets, or sending a change of address to a magazine. The main advantage of postcards is the fact that they don't have to be opened. They save a great deal of time for the companies that receive them.

Usually a blank postal card is already stamped and only requires a message, the address of the sender, and the address of the receiver. This type of card leaves the entire back available for the message. The front resembles a regular envelope. It has space for the receiver's address and the sender's address. If there is a problem with the delivery, the post office can return this type of card to the sender. Here is an example of a postal card:

Aunt Deda,

Mom and I plan to arrive in Arizona around the week of the Fourth of July. Could we visit you? It's been a long time since we have seen you and Uncle Clarence. I am looking forward to seeing how much the twins have grown and what your new house looks like. We can stay only a day or two, but it wouldn't seem right traveling all that way without stopping to say hello. If it isn't convenient for you to have us, please let us know. See you in a few months.

Love,

Alvin

Alvin Benton
185 Timber Blvd.
Seville MI 48832

Mrs. Diedra Campbell
84 Sunset Terrace
San Carlos AZ 85550

Reread the two examples of postcards on pages 14 and 15. Then answer the questions that follow.

1. What does the postal code AK stand for?

_____

2. In what state does Alvin Benton live?

_____

3. What does the abbreviation *Blvd* mean?

_____

4. Is Aunt Deda the sender or the receiver of the postcard?

_____

5. What is the full name of the person to whom Andy is writing?

_____

6. What city has the ZIP code 85550?

_____

7. In what state does Diedra Campbell live?

_____

8. What does the abbreviation *Dr* mean on Andy's postcard?

_____

9. What is on the front of Andy's postcard?

_____

10. Who wrote the postcard to Juan?

_____

11. What is the closing on the postcard Alvin wrote?

_____

12. Who wrote about a bowling team?

_____

A congratulatory letter is a useful way to show your happiness for friends and acquaintances who have had an important occasion in their lives. These notes can express your best wishes for a specific occasion, such as a birthday, new job, promotion, or honor. The opening line should state clearly the reason for your letter. For example:

> The girls in my scout troop are excited
> to hear that you were named Volunteer
> of the Year.

The rest of the letter follows the form of a friendly letter. The tone you choose depends on whether you wish to be formal or informal. If you know the receiver well, you will probably prefer to be informal. However, if you are not well acquainted with the receiver, you may wish to use more formal language. Consider these two models of tone:

> Gee, Nancy, I am so proud of your trophy!
> (informal)

> We are delighted to hear that your family has been selected to attend
> the regional conferences at Mt. Kisseck.
> (formal)

Here is an example of the first draft of a congratulatory letter. Read it and decide where it needs improvement.

385 Lantern Lane
Naples, Florida 33940
January 15, 1999

Dear Mrs. Zachary,
    My parents and I want to congratulate you on the adoption of a baby. We hope that you will visit us soon.

Yours,
Kim Voncannon

Notice that the letter is short because it lacks details. It is so short that it contains little warmth or sincere feeling. The closing is much too short to make the receiver feel that Kim is truly happy for her and her new baby. Rather, it almost sounds as though Kim's parents forced her to write the letter or that she didn't put much thought into it. The sample below is an improved version of the same letter on the previous page.

> 385 Lantern Lane
> Naples, Florida 33940
> January 15, 1999
>
> Dear Mrs. Zachary,
>
>   My parents and I are so pleased to hear that you and Mr. Zachary have adopted a baby girl. It is especially nice that you have named her April, which is Mother's first name. We hope that you and Mr. Zachary will bring April to visit us soon so that we can get to know her.
>
>   With much love,
>
>   *Kim Voncannon*

As you can see, this second version has included additional details in the body, which give the letter a sincere, thoughtful tone. In addition, the closing was changed to sound more personal and affectionate. Notice that the tone is formal, which is appropriate because a younger person is addressing an adult rather than a classmate or friend.

A Fill in the following letter with specific details about Larry's success in the annual bicycle race. Supply information and punctuation where necessary. Use Larry's name in the greeting.

776 _____

Sherburne, New York 13460

August _____ , 1999

Dear _____

    I am so pleased to hear about your _____

_____

_____

_____

_____

_____

_____

_____

_____

_____

_____

_____

_____

_____

_____

_____

_____

                                            _____

                                            _____

B Complete the envelope that follows with information you have copied from the above letter. Use the address you made up in the heading and the name you used in the closing for the sender's name, street, city, state, and ZIP code. Remember to replace the state name with a postal code. Make up a last name and an address for Larry, the receiver. Don't forget to draw in a stamp.

```
_____

_____

_____



                              _____

                              _____

                              _____
```

C Mark the following statements about congratulatory letters *True* or *False*.

_____ 1. Congratulatory letters always contain a sender's address.

_____ 2. The sender of a congratulatory letter should name specific details.

_____ 3. A comma always follows the greeting in a congratulatory letter.

_____ 4. The tone of a congratulatory letter must be formal.

_____ 5. The opening line of a congratulatory letter should state the sender's reason for writing.

_____ 6. A congratulatory letter expresses a person's best wishes for someone else's accomplishments or special occasions.

_____ 7. No closing is used in a congratulatory letter.

_____ 8. A congratulatory letter should be as short as you can make it.

Invitations

One of the most enjoyable uses of the mail is sending invitations. These messages range from short, handwritten announcements of small get-togethers or parties to the more formal, printed invitations for large dress-up affairs, such as weddings. Whatever the occasion, most people are glad to receive invitations because they signal a good time with friends.

Informal Invitations

When you compose an invitation to a small party or informal reception, all important information is usually placed in a single sentence. This information includes the name of the occasion, the date, the place, and the time. When the invitation represents a group, the sender should include a name and telephone number to which the receiver may reply. Additional sentences may suggest that the guest bring a food item or gift, or may provide useful information such as what clothes to wear for the occasion.

Here is an example of an informal invitation:

9063 Belton Avenue
Sayre, PA 18840
November 13, 1999

Dear Mr. Jamison,

The Prospectors' Club would enjoy having you drop by for their annual rock display this Saturday at the meeting hall of the Foundation Center, 167 Timberlane Way, from 4:00–7:00 P.M. If you need directions, please call me at 555-6089.

Sincerely,

Tony Oster

A Read the following invitation. Supply specific information to complete each blank.

877 Wendover Lane
Salem, Oregon 97301
May 25, 1999

Dear Chet,

We hope that you and your **(a)** _____ can come to

our **(b)** _____ and barbecue at our house, this

(c) _____, May 30, from noon until 7:00 **(d)** _____.

Please wear casual clothes and bring your **(e)** _____. This

should be a fun beginning-of-summer bash for the whole neighborhood!

(f) _____ ,
Derek McDougall

Formal Invitations

For more formal gatherings, such as wedding or anniversary receptions, openings of new restaurants, or large dinners, the host or hostess sends each guest an invitation engraved on a printed card or note. These invitations contain fewer words than a social letter—usually only the name, occasion, date, time, and place. Sometimes the lines are centered, as in the following model:

Mr. and Mrs. L. C. Richards, Jr.,
request the honor of your presence
at a New Year's Day buffet
on Tuesday, January 1,
at 11:30 A.M.
1853 Rhodale Place Northwest
Metairie, Louisiana

B Following the example on page 22, write a formal invitation to a victory party for a newly elected senator. Supply all the appropriate information. Center your lines.

_____

_____

_____

_____

_____

_____

_____

C Mark the following statements about invitations *True* or *False*.

_____ 1. Formal printed invitations are always signed in ink by the host.

_____ 2. All invitations should tell the occasion, place, time, and date.

_____ 3. An informal invitation should always tell you what kind of clothes to wear.

_____ 4. An informal invitation may have each line centered and engraved on a card.

_____ 5. Informal invitations follow the style of a friendly letter.

Accepting an Invitation

A host or hostess needs some idea of number of guests to expect. Also, the host should know whether the invitations have been received. The receiver of an invitation should respond immediately with a definite acceptance or rejection letter. Sometimes the invitation will include a card marked R.S.V.P., standing for the French phrase "Répondez, s'il vous plaît," meaning "Please reply."

The R.S.V.P. card provides the following important information:
➤ a line to mark whether the receiver will or will not attend the gathering
➤ the date by which it should be mailed
The thoughtful guest always returns this card promptly to let the sender know how many people are planning to attend.

If there is no card, a written acceptance letter restates the occasion, date, time, and place to show that the receiver understands the basic information.

---

770 Lime Street
Honolulu, Hawaii 96826
October 17, 1999

Dear Miss Tanaka,

My two sisters and I are pleased that we can attend Marshall's violin recital on Thursday, February 24, at 7:00 P.M. at Driscoll Musical Hall. We look forward to seeing you there.

Sincerely,

Cecil Ames

D On a separate piece of paper, compose an acceptance letter for an invitation to a masquerade ball at the local civic center. Make up details (place, time, date, your desire to attend) for your acceptance. Complete the assignment with an appropriate envelope. Be sure to use postal codes and abbreviations correctly. Draw a stamp in the upper right-hand corner.

Refusing an Invitation

Sometimes you may not want to attend a gathering. Other times you may be unable to go because of another invitation or responsibility. In these situations, a letter refusing the invitation must be more carefully worded than an acceptance letter. The opening sentence still states occasion, date, time, and place as in earlier models. Then, to spare any hurt feelings or misunderstandings, give a reason for the refusal in the next sentence. Read the model on the next page.

1005 Weyland Plaza
Lenox, Georgia 31637
June 20, 1999

Dear Mr. Turkelson,

    I am sorry that I will not be able to attend the reception honoring your visiting sisters at Eaton Memorial Gardens on Wednesday, July 2, at 2:00 P.M. My parents and I are going to be in Atlanta for a medical appointment. I regret that I will not meet your sisters at this time, but maybe I will see them before they return to Memphis.

                                     Yours sincerely,

                                     Margaret Anne Stein

E On a separate sheet of paper, rewrite the following refusal letter. Improve the organization and tone of the letter so that you avoid hurt feelings or misunderstandings. Supply any missing information.

844 Cornell Boulevard
Fredericksburg, Virginia 22401
March 3, 1999

Dear Mrs. Rodriguez,

    I am disappointed that I cannot attend on March 21. Thanks anyway for inviting me.

                                       Yours,

                                     Jeffrey Johnson, Jr.

Thank-You Notes

Thank-you notes can be sent for many reasons—after receiving a surprise graduation gift, going on a fishing trip with the neighbors, or visiting friends in a distant city. You should send your thanks in written form. This letter should resemble a friendly letter. However, it should be short and simple.

The opening line should state exactly what you are thanking your friends for, whether it be a Thanksgiving dinner, a bouquet of birthday flowers, tickets to a soccer match, or a trip to your best friend's summer cabin at the beach. Use these as models:

> My family is still enjoying the baked ham you brought last Sunday.

> I can't thank you enough for thinking of me with the copy of Emily Dickinson's poems from the library book sale.

> Last weekend at your family's lake lot was a terrific treat!

The second sentence should concentrate on your response to the gift. A good way to tell the sender that you liked the gift is to tell something about the gift that pleased you or how you plan to use it. For example:

> The green felt hat is just my size and is my favorite color.

> The twelve decorated cupcakes really made my birthday special.

> I can't wait to spend my gift certificate on a new desk lamp.

You should show your sincere thanks as warmly as possible, even if you received something that you do not need or want. Read the following thank-you notes to decide which version is superior.

2167 Walton Street
Compton, Maryland 20627
August 7, 1999

Dear Graingers,

    My scout troop thanks you for the use of your boat dock. You are very generous to Troop 119.

Yours,

Peter Rogers, Scoutmaster

In the thank-you note on page 26, notice that the sender has lumped the two people together in the greeting. Also, he omits details about the occasion as well as what he enjoyed about using the boat dock. The closing is proper, but it lacks warmth. Now read the improved version:

2167 Walton Street
Compton, Maryland 20627
August 7, 1999

Dear John and Allison,

    My fellow scouts and I appreciate the use of your boat dock for our annual outing. We enjoyed being able to swim, fish, and cook out together in a convenient location. You are very generous to Troop 119.

                  Many thanks,

                  Peter Rogers, Scoutmaster

A On a separate sheet of paper, compose your own thank-you note using the following facts. Grandfather Hughes gave Loretta a bracelet watch on her sixteenth birthday to mark improvement in her math grades. Supply any facts that you are missing.

B Select a phrase to complete each of the following sentences. Place the letter of your answer in the blank. You will have answers left over when you finish.

_____ 1. The first sentence of a thank-you note should _____.

_____ 2. A thank-you note should resemble _____.

_____ 3. The second sentence should concentrate on _____.

_____ 4. A thank-you letter should remain _____.

_____ 5. After a weekend visit, gift, or special occasion, _____.

a. a formal invitation
b. a friendly letter
c. state exactly what you are giving thanks for
d. place, time, and date
e. short and simple
f. your response to the gift
g. you may want to send your thanks in written form
h. a written thank-you is not necessary

Perhaps the hardest letter to write is a note of sympathy. Putting sad thoughts into words can be difficult. Sympathy notes should say exactly what you feel about the death of a person, a tragic accident, a house fire, or some other personal loss. A few short statements covering your emotional response is usually the best way to complete the job. State the reason for your sympathy in the first line. Read the following model to identify the reason for sympathy.

Apt. F, Mallard Cove
Greenville, Maine 04441
May 18, 1999

Dear Mrs. Conley,

    The news about Mr. Conley's death has saddened us all. He was a friend to every member of the Greenville Glee Club. We will certainly miss him.

With love,

Betty Jacobson

A Supply brief answers to the following questions.

1. In what state does Mrs. Conley live?

_____

2. What does the abbreviation *Apt.* stand for?

_____

3. Who is writing to Mrs. Conley?

_____

4. At what activity did Betty see Mr. Conley?

_____

5. With what words does Betty close her letter?

_____

6. How does Betty summarize her emotional response to Mr. Conley's death?

_____

7. What is the ZIP code for Greenville?

_____

8. To whom is the note written?

_____

9. How does Betty say the members of the glee club will feel in the future?

_____

10. Why was the note written?

_____

B Compose your own sympathy note, using the facts that follow.
Supply any facts that are missing.

Ms. Johnson, your favorite teacher, was in a serious automobile accident
and will be confined to the hospital for several weeks.

Review Unit 1

Use this section of your workbook to review the concepts that were introduced in lessons one through seven of your Friendly Letters unit. This will give you many opportunities to practice analyzing and writing friendly letters.

Friendly Letter Format

A Read the letter below. Identify the six lettered parts. If you have difficulty, refer to page 7.

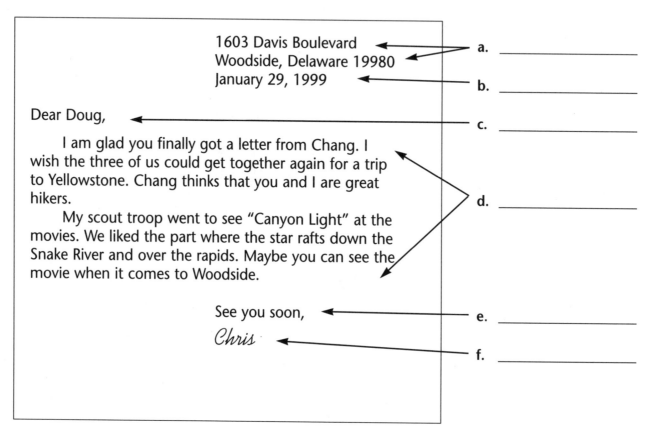

1603 Davis Boulevard
Woodside, Delaware 19980
January 29, 1999

a. _____

b. _____

Dear Doug,

c. _____

I am glad you finally got a letter from Chang. I wish the three of us could get together again for a trip to Yellowstone. Chang thinks that you and I are great hikers.

My scout troop went to see "Canyon Light" at the movies. We liked the part where the star rafts down the Snake River and over the rapids. Maybe you can see the movie when it comes to Woodside.

d. _____

See you soon,

e. _____

Chris

f. _____

Postal Codes and Abbreviations

B Write out in whole words the following postal codes and abbreviations. If you have difficulty, refer to page 10.

1. _____ Hdqrs.

2. _____ WY

3. _____ Ms.

4. _____ P.O.

5. _____ RI

6. _____ Ct.

7. _____ Rte.

8. _____ UT

9. _____ Bldg.

10. _____ Prov.

Letters, Envelopes, and Postcards

C Place items from the following lists under the headings where they belong. You may repeat items.

body   date   greeting
receiver's address   closing   signature
stamp   sender's address

Letters	Envelopes	Picture postcards

Notes of Invitation (Formal and Informal), Thank-You Notes, Congratulatory Notes, and Sympathy Notes

D Decide in what kind of letter you would find the following opening sentences. Write your answer on the blank line.

1. My club would love to have your band play for the Easter weekend banquet.

   _____

2. Congratulations on the award the band won for their part in the mall opening.

   _____

3. Leah and I appreciated your help with the art display last Saturday.

   _____

4. My family is sorry to hear that your pony died in the flood.

   _____

5. The Central Bank requests the honor of your presence at a postgame brunch on Sunday, April 4, 1999, at 10:30 A.M.

   _____

Friendly Letter Writing

E On a separate sheet of paper, compose a body of a letter to fit each of these situations.

1. You have enjoyed the use of a friend's sleeping bag for a trip to Linville Gorge.

2. Your family wishes to invite your teacher to a barbecue to honor family and friends.

3. Your neighbor has won a promotion to vice president of a local landscaping company.

4. You are issuing printed invitations to a 25th anniversary party for a barbershop quartet.

5. You want to express your sorrow for the death of a friend's younger brother in a car accident.

Envelope Writing

F In the space below, prepare an envelope. Use your own address for that of the sender. Make up an address for the receiver. Draw a stamp in the correct place.

Unit Test

Friendly Letter Format

A Below are examples of the parts of a friendly letter. Write the name of each letter part.

1. _____ Dear Maria,

2. _____ 41 Oak Lane

Danby, Vermont 05739

3. _____ Your sister,

4. _____ December 12, 1999

5. _____ I miss you since you have gone to college.

6. _____ Juanita

Envelope Format

B Write the following information on the envelope. Be sure to capitalize and punctuate correctly. Draw a stamp where it should be.

Sender: connie mills
    25 central street
    silverton idaho 83867

Receiver: mr robert allen
    122 sands avenue
    selma alabama 36702

1. _____

2. _____

3. _____

4. _____

5. _____

6. _____

Types of Friendly Letters

C Decide in what kind of friendly letter you would find each of the following sentences. Write the letter on the line.

a. basic friendly letter	**d.** formal invitation	**g.** thank-you note
b. postcard	**e.** informal invitation	**h.** sympathy note
c. note of congratulations	**f.** reply to an invitation	

_____ 1. Sara and I appreciated the loan of your canoe.

_____ 2. Congratulations on winning the beach volleyball championship match.

_____ 3. We are staying at the hotel on the front of the card.

_____ 4. The Art League invites you to a special exhibit of watercolors on March 15, 1999, at 7 P.M. at the Gibson Gallery.

_____ 5. I have been meaning to write you about my new school, but I just haven't had the time.

_____ 6. Dan and I are sorry we will not be able to attend your son's wedding on June 16, 1999, at 10:00 A.M.

_____ 7. Our family was sorry to hear that your garage was destroyed by fire.

_____ 8. We hope you will be able to come to Brianna's birthday party.

Writing Friendly Letters

D Choose one of the situations below. On a separate sheet of paper, write a complete letter.

1. You want to tell your grandmother about the guitar lessons you have been taking.

2. Your family is having a party for Cinco de Mayo and you want to invite your friend Hector.

3. You feel sad when you find out your neighbor has died and you want to tell his wife how sorry you are.

4. Your aunt and uncle sent you computer software for your birthday and you want to thank them.

5. Your teacher has been promoted to vice-principal and you want to congratulate her.

Business Letters

Writing business letters is not a job just for secretaries, executives, politicians, or salespeople. Everyone conducts business of some type, such as placing mail orders, applying for membership, giving instructions, explaining an absence to a teacher or employer, ordering magazine subscriptions, joining civic clubs, or expressing opinions. Many of these tasks require formal written communication.

Business letters differ from friendly letters in the following ways:
➤ are strictly informative
➤ avoid emotion or personal responses
➤ concentrate on facts
➤ are short and to the point
➤ are always typed or written in black or blue ink
  on standard stationery that is 8 1/2" x 11"

A business letter may be an announcement about when a conference is taking place, a request for payment, an order for a shipment of goods, an announcement of a club activity, or a statement of customer dissatisfaction with a product. Business letters may also ask for more information, explain a difficult situation, or reply to a proposal. Generally, business letters are typed using a computer or a typewriter.

Letter Style

Business letters follow a style different from that of friendly letters. There are three variations of the basic business-letter style—**semiblock, block,** and **full block.** Any of these three arrangements is acceptable, depending upon what you or your company prefers. Often an individual will select a style that is personally pleasing. Other people vary the style they choose, depending upon the length of the letter.

Spacing is important in a business letter. It should always be edged with a one-inch margin. If it is written on letterhead stationery, the writer may skip several inches before beginning. Study the model of semiblock letter style that follows. Notice that in the semiblock style, every line except the heading, closing, signature, and paragraph indentions begins at the left margin.

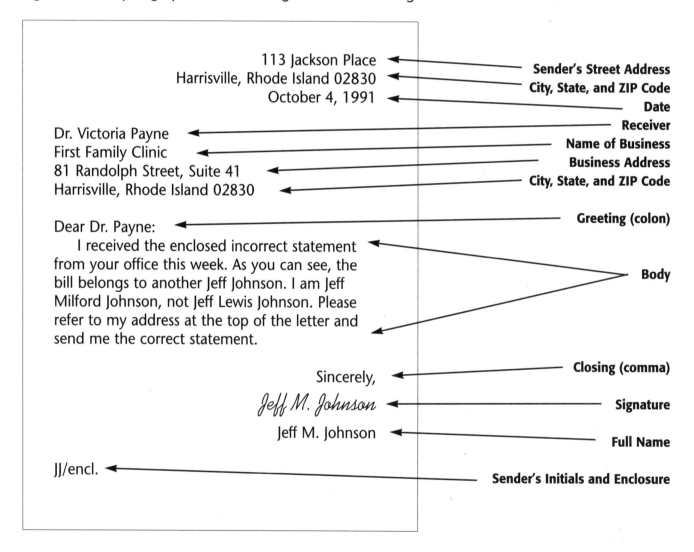

The basic structure of a business letter includes the heading, the inside address, the greeting, the body, the closing, and the signature. Notice that there are some details in the model business letter that do not appear in a friendly letter.

➤ Heading

The sender's address goes in the same place as in a friendly letter, that is, at the right at the top of the letter. If the sender represents a company, that information appears on the first line. It is followed by the mailing address, city and state, ZIP code, and date. For example:

> GAC Implements, Inc.
> P.O. Box 8078
> Bliss, Idaho 83314
> December 6, 1999

➤ Inside Address

Two lines below and to the left of the sender's address is the receiver's name and address. If the receiver has a title, it appears after the name. A comma separates the title from the name. The name of the receiver is followed by the name of the business, mailing address, city and state, and ZIP code. For example:

> Rhoda Blakesley, Executive Assistant
> Virginia Board of Tourism
> 2128 Stonewall Avenue, Suite 60
> Richmond, Virginia 23250

➤ Greeting

The greeting in a business letter is followed by a colon (:). The greeting itself should avoid informality by addressing the receiver by name or title. For example:

> Members of the board:
> To the Personnel Manager:
> Dear Dr. Samuels:

➤ Body

The body of a business letter often has three main parts. The first part briefly introduces the subject of the letter. The second part should name all details that are important to the matter discussed. Finally, in the third part, the letter writer should sum up what is expected, such as the correction of an error, the mailing of a parcel, or a change in company policy. If the letter is long, these three segments should be stated in three separate paragraphs.

➤ Closing

The closing is in the same place as in a friendly letter. It is followed by a comma. Unlike a friendly letter, the closing in a business letter should not emphasize personal emotions. For example:

> Sincerely,
> Respectfully,
> With regards,
> With gratitude,

➤ **Signature**

Directly beneath the closing is the signature. Unlike a friendly letter, a business letter contains the writer's full name typed or printed neatly under the signature. This rewriting helps to clarify illegible handwriting. If the writer has a title, it appears in a separate line under the name.

➤ **Reference Initials**

The last line on a business letter gives the receiver important information. First, as shown in the model, the initials "JJ" indicate that Jeff Johnson typed his own letter. If another person had typed it for him, the initials "JJ" would have been followed by a slash and the typist's initials, for example, "JJ/mes." A second important piece of information that may appear at the end of the letter is the abbreviation "encl.," which shows that something is enclosed in the envelope with the letter, such as a list, contract, or statement of charges.

Another abbreviation beneath the signature is "cc," which stands for *carbon copy.* ("pc"—photocopy) If copies of the letter have been sent to other people, their names will appear with the abbreviation in this form:

  cc: Janice Raymond, Comptroller
  pc: R. D. Ingersoll, Technical Director

A Supply a word or phrase to complete these statements about the model semiblock letter. Select answers from the list below. Answers will be left over when you finish.

body	full block	city and state	initials
colon	JJ	emotions	receiver's
business	signature	date	title
encl.	computer	facts	

1. A _____ is the proper punctuation to use after the greeting in a business letter.

2. A business letter contains both the sender's and the _____ addresses.

3. The abbreviation _____ means that something is enclosed in the letter.

4. Both a _____ and the sender's full name appear after the closing in a business letter.

5. The sender's _____ appear on the bottom left-hand line of a business letter.

6. The receiver's _____ is named on the line after the receiver's name in the inside address.

7. If the receiver has a _____, it appears after the name and is separated from the name by a comma.

8. Business letters are usually typed on a _____ or typewriter.

9. Business communications concentrate on _____ rather than emotional responses.

10. The style of a business letter may be semiblock, _____, or block.

11. The _____ of a typical letter generally has three main parts.

12. The closing of a business letter is followed by a comma and does not emphasize

   personal _____.

B Read the following list of elements in a business letter. Underline the elements that are necessary in friendly letters.

date	sender's initials	signature
sender's address	receiver's address	greeting
full name of sender	body	receiver's title
receiver's name	receiver's company	colon
sender's city and state	receiver's city and state	comma
closing	sender's ZIP code	

C Place the following items in the order in which they appear in a business letter. Record your answers on the lines below. Omit any items that do not belong in a business letter.

date	sender's initials	signature
sender's street address	receiver's ZIP code	greeting
emotional response	full name of sender	body
receiver's name	receiver's business	colon after greeting
sender's city and state	receiver's city and state	comma
closing	sender's ZIP code	receiver's title
encl.	cc	paragraph indention

1. _____

2. _____

3. _____

4. _____

5. _____

6. _____

7. _____

8. _____

9. _____

10. _____

11. _____

12. _____

13. _____

14. _____

15. _____

16. _____

17. _____

18. _____

19. _____

20. _____

D Write an example for each requested item.

1. Heading for a business letter   _____
   (use your address)   _____
      _____

2. Inside address for a business letter   _____
   (make up a business name and address)   _____
      _____

3. Greeting for a business letter   _____
   (punctuate it)

4. Closing for a business letter   _____
   (punctuate it)

Envelopes for Business Letters

The size of envelope in which a business letter is sent is similar to that of the envelope for a friendly letter; however, the envelope may be longer so that long legal documents and forms will fit inside it. The sender's address goes in the upper left-hand corner. The sender's name and title, if the sender has one, is written on the first line. The name of the sender's company, again, if there is one, is written under the sender's name.

The receiver's name, title, company name, street address, city, state, and ZIP code go in the lower right-hand section of the envelope. If the letter requires the attention of a particular businessperson, that name follows the abbreviation "ATTN" and a colon in the lower left-hand corner. Don't forget the stamp.

E Complete the model envelope for a business letter. Use information from the list. Some answer choices will not be used.

Andrew	Manager	Blvd.	MO
Dr.	142	West Market St.	40380
School	Jr.	Stanton	encl.
Sender	Manufacturing	Colon	Jones

Mrs. Adrian Lackey, **(a)** _____

Porter Secretarial **(b)** _____

(c) _____

Urbana **(d)** _____ 65767

Mr. **(e)** _____ Jones, President

ABC **(f)** _____ Company

Box 43-C Old Barn Road

(g) _____ KY **(h)** _____

ATTN: Mr. Andrew **(i)** _____

The Block Style Letter

The block style letter is similar to the semiblock style. The main difference is that there are no indentions at each paragraph. To show the change from one paragraph to another, the writer must skip one line. All other elements in the letter remain the same. Both letters communicate the same information. The two styles merely represent differences in taste.

F Rewrite the following information in block style. Place your letter on a separate sheet of paper.

800 Marshall Street
New York, New York 10016
March 27, 1999

Mr. R. Carlton Stamey, President
Westby Theaters, Inc.
1880 Union Plaza
Wichita, Kansas 67216

Dear Sir:

I read your advertisement in the *Daily Tribune* for a manager of the new Westby Theater in my area. I am interested in applying for the job. My qualifications include experience managing a skating rink. Before that, I worked four years as the assistant manager of a lumberyard.

Enclosed is a copy of my educational background and work record. If you still need a manager, I would appreciate the opportunity to interview for the position.

Yours sincerely,

Joseph T. Ruggles

Joseph T. Ruggles
Manager
Cranford Skating Rink

JR/encl.

Full Block Style

The third style of business letter is called full block. The full block style differs from block style in the placement of the sender's address, the closing, the signature, and the full name. All information in full block style—the sender's address, receiver's address, greeting, body, closing, signature, full name, and sender's initials—is aligned at the left-hand margin. Because the paragraphs begin at the left and there is no indention, the writer must skip one line between the paragraphs. Consider this example of a letter that uses the full block style:

---

48 Central Boulevard
Woodstock, Vermont 05091
April 16, 1999

Dr. Lance Chronister, General Manager
State Accounting Office
Box 1145-C
Tallahassee, Florida 32303

Dear Dr. Chronister:

I am writing a report on state accounting procedures for my high school class in business administration. I would like to buy a copy of your service manual. Please send all necessary ordering information to the above address.

With appreciation,

Sandra Alston

Sandra Alston

SA

G Compose a short letter to a company suggesting a change in a product that you like, such as bath gel, microwave popcorn, or sports shoes. Write your letter in semiblock, block, and full block style. Study the appearance of each letter. Then decide which style suits your taste. Address an envelope to accompany the letter.

UNIT 2

Excuse Letter

Many short letters require a particular style to suit their purpose. One type of letter that a student may write is an excuse for an absence or tardiness. This note may or may not have to be signed by both the writer and a doctor, parent, or guardian. The form for an excuse letter is briefer than that for a normal business letter. It need not include the sender's and receiver's addresses.

An excuse letter should begin with the date and continue through the signature. It does not require the sender's full name or initials. Use of an envelope is optional. If the excuse is hand delivered, there is no need for an envelope. If, however, it must be left on a desk or in a mailbox, it should be placed in an envelope. The receiver's name should be written on the front of the envelope.

A Using the following facts, compose a work excuse. Write your finished letter on the blank lines below. Supply all necessary punctuation. Begin with today's date. Use a semiblock style.

Gayle McNeill
illness in the family
missed a half day's work

Mrs. Jeffers
Thursday morning
central office of Walton Granary Works

Dear _____:

_____

_____

_____

_____

_____

Sincerely yours,

_____

Apology Letter

Often it is necessary to handle differences between people or unpleasant situations by means of a business letter. Unlike the excuse letter, a note of apology should include all aspects of the business letter. It should be factual and free of heavy emotion.

Begin an apology letter by clearly stating the situation that needs clarifying. For example, you may need to apologize for damaging a notebook, misstating facts, or losing your temper in a business meeting. After this explanation, make your apology brief. For example:

RFD 10, Box 27-B
Two Rivers, Wisconsin 54247
May 12, 1999

Mrs. Constance McClamrock, Night Clerk
Richardson Hotel
542 Highway 45
Big Springs, West Virginia 26137

Dear Mrs. McClamrock:

From May 5–10 I was a guest at the Richardson Hotel. During my last night of occupancy, I accidentally picked up a brown sweater from the hotel lobby among my packages. The manager informs me that the sweater belongs to you. I am returning your sweater by UPS this morning. You can expect it in a few days. I am sorry to have inconvenienced you.

Respectfully,

Jack Denton

Jack Denton

JD/gbw

B On a separate sheet of paper and using full block style, write a letter of apology based on the following situation: While spending the night at the house of a friend, you carelessly stained a new sofa.

C Choose words or phrases from the letter of apology on page 45 to answer the questions below.

1. In what state is the Richardson Hotel?

_____

2. What is Jack Denton's ZIP code?

_____

3. What word in the body of the letter means *annoyed* or *troubled?*

_____

4. What is Mrs. McClamrock's official title at the hotel?

_____

5. On what days did Mr. Denton stay at the Richardson Hotel?

_____

6. By what means is he returning the sweater?

_____

7. What initials tell you that Jack Denton did not type his own letter of apology?

_____

8. How long after his stay at the hotel did Jack Denton write his letter of apology?

_____

9. Who told Jack Denton to whom the sweater belonged?

_____

10. When was the sweater picked up?

_____

Instructive Letter

Often a business letter must give tedious information about the use of a machine, a lengthy and perplexing route, a complex medical or dental procedure, a manufacturing process, or some other itemized list of instructions or details. This type of letter often numbers the individual items in the list to make it easier for the receiver to follow the instructions. For example:

Phillips Electronics Company
71 Willoughby Circle
Dixon, Wyoming 82323
October 10, 1999

Professor R. L. Kurtz
Mason Central College
2109 Lansing Way
Charlottesville, Indiana 46117

Dear Sir:

My firm has received your complaint about the lighted magnifying glass that you purchased from our spring catalog. I regret that you are having difficulty focusing the light on your work. Perhaps I can help with the following suggestions:

1. Attach the lamp base to a soft surface that the clamp can grasp. If necessary, wrap the surface in a terry towel.
2. Steady the extension arm with one hand while tightening the bolt with the other. Don't force it.
3. When you have the bulb focused to best advantage, tighten the leveling device, which holds the shade in place.

If these procedures are unsuccessful, don't hesitate to call me at 1-800-555-3311. I may be able to save you further disappointment with the product.

Respectfully,

Len Daye

Len Daye
Quality Control Engineer

LD/apm

D Mark the following statements about the model instructive letter on page 47 either *True* or *False*.

_____ 1. Len Daye probably works as a college professor.

_____ 2. The ZIP code for the sender's address is 82323.

_____ 3. Len Daye typed his own letter.

_____ 4. This letter is written in block style.

_____ 5. The extension arm should be steadied before the base is clamped to a soft surface.

_____ 6. The company will reimburse Professor Kurtz's money if the lamp proves unsatisfactory.

_____ 7. According to the inside address, Charlottesville is in Indiana.

_____ 8. The instructive list is a part of paragraph 1.

_____ 9. A telephone call to Len Daye is free.

E Address the following envelope for a letter of reply from Professor Kurtz to Len Daye. Include an attention line to the receiver. Draw a stamp where it belongs.

F On a separate piece of paper, compose a letter of instruction to another student, explaining how to write a business letter. Then copy your letter here.

_____

_____

_____

_____

_____

_____

_____

_____:

_____

_____

_____

_____

_____

_____

_____

_____

_____,

_____

Letters from a Group

Another type of business letter that requires special attention is a letter written by one person but representing the sentiments of an entire group, such as a club, neighborhood, class, office, or community. For example, your school band may write to several companies asking for donations to cover the cost of a band workshop.

A letter from a group should begin with a clear statement of whose feelings or ideas are being represented. Even though the sentences speak for the group, the letter is signed by one spokesperson, for example, the secretary, the volunteer leader, or the office representative.

Consider this model of a letter from a group:

70061 Mill Valley Road
Baltic, Connecticut 06330
December 29, 1999

Dr. Joan Lail
Barringer Advertising Agency
112 Julian Avenue, Suite 68
Brighton, Massachusetts 02135

Dear Dr. Lail:

    The members of the Baltic Model Rocket Club would like to request your assistance in launching a membership drive. We understand that you specialize in helping small clubs with advertising problems.
    Our greatest need is for more active members. Could you suggest ways in which we could invite people who would have interest in the group? Do you have a pamphlet offering information about reorganization or membership drives for small clubs? I have enclosed a self-addressed stamped envelope for your reply.

        Many thanks,

        Barry M. Kirby

        Barry M. Kirby
        Secretary-Treasurer

BMK/encl.

■ Select a word or phrase from the letter on page 50 to answer each of the following questions.

1. In what state does the model club meet?

_____

2. Who is acting as the club's spokesperson?

_____

3. What is his title?

_____

4. Where does Dr. Lail work?

_____

5. What is the ZIP code of Baltic?

_____

6. In what style is this letter written?

_____

7. Where is Brighton located?

_____

8. What does the sender enclose in the envelope?

_____

9. Is Barry's middle name Matthew, Thomas, or Anthony?

_____

10. Where did you find the answer to question 9?

_____

11. How do you know that Barry typed his own letter?

_____

A special type of letter is a written reply to a published news article, feature, or editorial. A letter to the editor is a means of expressing your opinion on an issue, such as balancing the federal or state budget, banning smoking in public elevators and buses, increasing local sales taxes, or providing a swimming pool for the local recreation center. Letters to the editor usually appear on the editorial page in a special section of a newspaper or magazine.

A letter to the editor is beneficial to the community as a whole. The person writing the letter is interested in communicating not only with the editor, but also with the readers of a magazine or newspaper. By publishing a variety of responses to an issue, such as the expansion of a major highway or the reelection of a mayor or sheriff, the newspaper or magazine encourages public debate. By airing different opinions, the editor helps the public sample local feelings on the issues and understand public needs. Although issues are seldom settled to everyone's satisfaction, readers of letters to the editor are made aware of the more vocal supporters or opponents of an idea.

Like other letters in this section of the workbook, a letter to the editor should conform to business style and tone. It differs from other business letters in its greeting, which is "To the Editor." The body of the letter should remain factual and to the point. A letter to the editor should never libel or degrade other people. By focusing on the positive aspects of a single view of the issue, the letter makes a strong statement for or against the issue. For example, letters could be about the use of public landfills for toxic wastes, the establishment of a daycare center, or a campaign against noise at a nearby airport. A letter to the editor should end in a clear summary statement, leaving no doubt of the writer's opinion.

When planning a letter to the editor, be sure you know what your opinion is and think it is worth defending. Readers of the letter may be more willing to accept your opinion if it is supported with convincing evidence and facts. Make a list of possible reasons for your opinion and facts that support it. Then use the best or most effective in the letter. Remember that emotional opinions based solely on personal preferences are not very persuasive. Although a writer might feel strongly about an issue, emotional outbursts should be avoided, for they often distract readers from the real issues.

If an argument or opinion is going to be supported by more than one point or argument, transition words such as *first, next, last, another example,* or *in addition* can be used to help guide the reader. Study the example of a letter to the editor on page 53.

6671 Bentley Place
Medford, Minnesota 56049
January 4,1999

Roseanne Wysocki, City Editor
The Medford Times-Dispatch
One Main Street
Medford, Minnesota 56049

To the Editor:

   For several weeks, the *Medford Times-Dispatch* has promoted local land developers who want to build a shopping mall south of town. My neighbors and I support these efforts. People living in the southern end of Medford have a difficult time traveling by car or bus to the center of town to shop. The convenience of a suburban mall would aid older shoppers as well as parents of young children. Another asset of a mall will be the boost to business, which is sorely needed in southern Medford. Everyone will profit when the shopping mall becomes a reality.

                                        Yours Sincerely,

                                        Pete Guerrera

                                        Pete Guerrera

PRG

A Complete the following exercises.

1. Discuss the two reasons that Pete Guerrera gives to support the building of a shopping mall in southern Medford.

a. _____

_____

b. _____

_____

2. Explain how Pete Guerrera ends his letter.

_____

_____

_____

3. Suggest some reasons why other people might not support the building of a shopping mall.

_____

_____

_____

B Choose words or phrases from the letter to the editor on page 53 to answer the following questions.

1. Who is the city editor of the local newspaper?

_____

2. Who typed the letter to the editor?

_____

3. How does the writer close his letter?

_____

4. Does the writer live in the town where the newspaper is located?

_____

5. What information gives you the answer to question 4?

_____

6. What other people agree with the writer's opinion?

_____

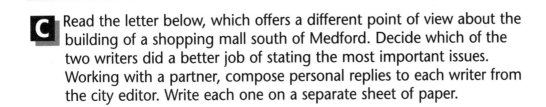

C Read the letter below, which offers a different point of view about the building of a shopping mall south of Medford. Decide which of the two writers did a better job of stating the most important issues. Working with a partner, compose personal replies to each writer from the city editor. Write each one on a separate sheet of paper.

Apt. 34-D, Grant Woods
Medford, Minnesota 56049
January 4, 1999

Roseanne Wysocki, City Editor
The Medford Times-Dispatch
One Main Street
Medford, Minnesota 56049

Dear Editor Wysocki:

My family and I have been reading your recent articles in the *Medford Times-Dispatch* about a possible shopping mall near our neighborhood. Already our lives have been disrupted by busy intersections and traffic that backs up all the way to Route 48. Mornings are so difficult for us that the children must get up a half hour earlier just to be on time for school.

Have the developers decided how they will stop traffic from blocking driveways? Has anybody asked them how school buses will get through the afternoon rush? Have city officials considered building a front entrance to the mall in another location?

My children and I want these matters discussed at the next meeting of the town council. We think Medford owes its students a safe and easy route to school before it starts building another mall.

Respectfully,

Mrs. Roberta Epps

Roberta Epps

RE

U N I T 2

Writing to a senator, representative, or other government or military official is another challenging form of a business letter. You may need to write this type of letter to express your opinion on a local matter, to ask for assistance, or to request an official brochure. Whatever your reason for writing to an official, you should state the purpose of the letter in the opening sentence. The next sentences should explain details as briefly, but as clearly, as possible. All references to the official should include his or her title, as in Senator Jane Allman or Representative Marcus R. Tatum, Jr.

For this area of business communication, you may need the following list of title abbreviations:

Adm.	Admiral	**Rep.**	Representative	**Gen.**	General
Lt.	Lieutenant	**Col.**	Colonel	**Supt.**	Superintendent
Atty.	Attorney	**Sec.**	Secretary	**Gov.**	Governor
Maj.	Major	**Com.**	Commissioner	**Treas.**	Treasurer
Capt.	Captain	**Sen.**	Senator	**Hon.**	Honorable
Pvt.	Private	**Ens.**	Ensign	**V. Pres.**	Vice-president
Cmdr.	Commander	**Sgt.**	Sergeant	**Amb.**	Ambassador

A Shorten the following names by abbreviating the titles. Write only the abbreviated title.

_____ 1. General Andrew S. Martin

_____ 2. Lee Dara, Secretary-Treasurer

_____ 3. Lieutenant Governor Sara Moore

_____ 4. Sergeant Alvis Tanner

_____ 5. Representative Luis Gonzalez

B Write out the words that the following abbreviations represent.

_____ 1. Com.   _____ 6. Cmdr.

_____ 2. Hon.   _____ 7. Sen.

_____ 3. Supt.   _____ 8. Sgt.

_____ 4. Col.   _____ 9. V. Pres.

_____ 5. Atty.   _____ 10. Adm.

C Using the following information, compose a letter in semiblock style: Governor P. L. Deane; public concern about the closing of exit ramps from a state highway; State Capitol; Suite 83; Lincoln, Nebraska 68501. Use your own name and address as the sender. Explain how you feel about the matter. Note that you are enclosing a map of state highways with the area marked in red. Also indicate that Rae Winstead typed the letter. Then prepare an envelope. Use the form below for the envelope.

_____

_____

_____

                                       _____

                                       _____

                                       _____

                                       _____

Mid-Unit Test

Business Letter Format

A Write the name of each part of the business letter shown below. Use the list to help you. Some choices will be left over.

heading   body   block   inside address   closing
typists   initials   greeting   signature   title

_____ **1.** Sincerely,

_____ **2.** Crafts, Incorporated

                        873 Clarke Street

                        Dallas, Texas 75214

_____ **3.** I am writing to ask your help for our Science Club.

_____ **4.** 72 East Valley Road

                        Kansas City, Missouri 64130

                        February 25, 1999

_____ **5.** To the Editor:

_____ **6.** Alice Morgan

_____ **7.** gmh

Business Letter Style

B Write *semiblock, block,* or *full block* to tell what style is used for each form.

1. _____   **2.** _____   **3.** _____

Writing Business Letters

C Write the inside address and the greeting for each set of information.

1. The Director of Personnel, Ms. Anne Jensen, at the Ames Aircraft Company, located in ZIP code 78840, in Del Rio, Texas, at 7284 Mesa Road

_____

_____

_____

_____

_____

2. Eastland State College located in Clifton, South Carolina, 2299 Bonner Drive, the Dean of Students, ZIP code 29324, Dr. Wilson Woodson

_____

_____

_____

_____

_____

Types of Business Letters

D Decide in what kind of business letter you would find the following opening sentences. Write the letter of the correct type on the line. You will not use all the choices shown in the list.

a. apology letter
b. instructional letter
c. excuse letter
d. letter from a group
e. letter to an official
f. letter to the editor

_____ 1. I am writing in response to a column in Tuesday's *Daily Herald.*

_____ 2. I am so sorry I forgot your birthday, Harold.

_____ 3. Our family would like to bring an important matter to your attention, Senator Brown.

_____ 4. My daughter, Sue, was absent yesterday because she was ill.

A business communication that almost everyone writes at some time is the job application. Often a person looking for work will find a blind advertisement in the newspaper. This item contains a box number but no other identifying information. For example:

WANTED

Refrigeration repair tech. 2 wk. vacation; health ins. Send appl., res., and sal. req. to Box 23, Dept. C.

To reply to a blind advertisement, address your letter to the newspaper. Be sure to use the box number mentioned in the advertisement. Study the following model letter from Specialist Fourth Class Wesley Timmons. It demonstrates how to reply to a blind advertisement of a job vacancy.

1666 Radnor Street
Ft. Dix, New Jersey 08640
May 11, 1999

Daily Gazette
P.O. Box 23, Dept. C
Ft. Dix, New Jersey 08640

To the Personnel Director:

    I am finishing a tour of duty in the U.S. Army. I am interested in finding a job in the Ft. Dix area. Your ad in the *Daily Gazette* sounds like work that I have been trained to do and that I enjoy. Since joining the Army in 1996, I have studied refrigeration repair and have been assigned to the base commissary. I would be pleased to interview for your advertised position as a refrigeration repair technician. I am looking for a salary in the $28,000 to $32,000 range. If you wish, you may reach me by telephone at this number (609) 555-0155, afternoons between 3:00 and 7:00 P.M. My résumé is enclosed.

                                 Yours respectfully,

                                 Sp4c Wesley Timmons

                                 Sp4c Wesley Timmons

WT/encl.

A Choose a word or phrase from the letter on page 60 to answer the questions below.

1. What do the following abbreviations stand for?

   Ft. _____   Dept. _____

   P.O. _____   Sp4c _____

2. Who is the receiver of the letter?

   _____

3. For what job does Wesley Timmons want to interview?

   _____

4. Is this letter written in semiblock, block, or full block style?

   _____

5. In what state does Wesley Timmons want to work?

   _____

6. What is the telephone area code of that state?

   _____

7. Where did you find the answer to question 6?

   _____

8. Where was the ad seen?

   _____

B Rewrite the above letter on page 60 in full block style. Replace the newspaper box number with the following receiver's name, company, street address, city, state, and ZIP code: Latham R. Sanders, President; Ace Refrigeration Repair; 8483 Mountain View Road.; Ft. Dix, New Jersey 08640. Place Mr. Sanders's name in the greeting. Write your letter on a separate piece of paper. Address an envelope to accompany it.

Preparing a Résumé

Most letters of application include a résumé. This document is a list of jobs and experiences that the applicant uses to prove his or her ability. The résumé may take a variety of forms, depending upon what the applicant wants to emphasize. The important thing to remember is that in a résumé you are trying to give a potential employer a reason for hiring you. You want to create a favorable impression. The basic structure of the résumé generally includes the following: background, education, work history, special interests, and references.

Background

The opening section of a résumé usually gives personal information, such as your full name, address, and telephone number. You may include your birth date. However, equal opportunity employment laws protect you from discrimination based on age, sex, race, religion, or national origin. You might also want to include your social security number.

Education

The résumé should list schools that you have attended along with the dates of enrollment and graduation. These are usually given in reverse order, beginning with the most recent and going back to high school. You should include information about diplomas received or certification in particular fields.

Work History

The third part of a résumé usually states all the places that you have been employed. This list, like the list of schools, is written in reverse order, beginning with the current job and going back to former jobs. Each job description should include the exact nature of your work as well as the dates of your employment. To highlight your stronger abilities and qualities, mention any awards or honors you may have received during your employment, such as a perfect attendance certificate or an outstanding employee award. If you have little or no work experience, list examples of volunteer work you have done or events you may have organized. For example, you might list that you were chairperson for a school book fair or that you work with senior citizens or tutor young children.

Special Interests

To give a full view of what kind of person you are, you may state your hobbies, interests, club and professional memberships, and other pastimes. If you have traveled widely, you might want to mention the places you have visited. If you have special skills, such as being able to speak more than one language, list them.

References

At the conclusion of your résumé, you should list two or three people to whom you are not related and who know your work and can verify that you are an honest and dependable person. On page 63, you will find an example of a résumé for Sp4c Wesley Timmons.

Sp4c Wesley Timmons
1666 Radnor Street
Ft. Dix, New Jersey 08640
(609) 555-0155

Education:

U.S. Army Refrigeration Training Center Ft. Dix, New Jersey Degree: A.A. in refrigeration and small appliance repair	June–August 1996
Southern Community College Atlanta, Georgia	1993–1995
Brunswick County High School Brunswick, Georgia Degree: Diploma	1989–1993

Work History:

Specialist Fourth Class U.S. Army, specializing in refrigeration	1996–1999
Assistant Produce Manager King's Food Store Recognition: Named Employee of the Month four times	1989–1996

Special Interests:
Certified Red Cross swimming and diving instructor
Watercolor and charcoal art

References:

Rev. Frank Graham Dunleavy
First Presbyterian Church
Brunswick, Georgia 31520

Dr. Annette Peeler
Freewood Medical Clinic
Route 601
Brunswick, Georgia 31520

Corley Dirks, Manager
King's Food Store
66 Main Street
Brunswick, Georgia 31520

U
N
I
T

2

C Using the model on page 63, prepare a résumé for yourself as you want it to read in 10 years. Include schools you would like to attend as well as jobs and hobbies that reflect your skills and interests. Use real references to people whom you know well.

_____

_____

_____

_____

Education:

_____   _____

_____

_____

_____   _____

_____

_____

Work History:

_____   _____

_____

_____

_____   _____

_____

_____

Special Interests:

_____

_____

_____

References:

_____   _____

_____   _____

_____   _____

_____   _____

Follow-Up Letters

In business dealings, it is both good manners and a wise business practice to follow up an interview or conference with a letter. This communication takes the form of a normal business letter. It states the purpose and outcome of the interview or conference. Also, the sender expresses thanks for any personal service, such as a job recommendation or promotion, or advice on educational plans. Read the model below of a follow-up letter to determine whether it is effective.

---

825 McGowan Court
Salisbury, North Carolina 28144
July 30, 1999

Francine Summers
Lakewood Industries
909 Terrace Boulevard
Raleigh, North Carolina 27606

Dear Ms. Summers:

Thank you so much for giving me the opportunity to interview for the job of your personal secretary. Your kindness and courtesy put me immediately at ease. If I am selected for the position, I will do my best to fill it well.

Sincerely,

Evelyn Vickers

Evelyn Vickers

EV

Notice that the first draft is missing several important details. The inside address does not list the receiver's title. The body of the letter does not state important details that might make all the difference in who actually gets the job. For example, the writer should mention what experience she has in office work and how her secretarial training has prepared her for the job. She should also be specific about why she would like to have this particular job and why she would be a good candidate for it.

Finally, to conclude well, the writer should show more appreciation for the interview, which may result in a new job for her. Consider this improved version of the first letter.

825 McGowan Court
Salisbury, North Carolina 28144
July 30, 1999

Francine Summers, Personnel Manager
Lakewood Industries
909 Terrace Boulevard
Raleigh, North Carolina 27606

Dear Ms. Summers:

Thank you so much for giving me the opportunity to interview for the job of your personal secretary. Your kindness and courtesy put me immediately at ease.

I feel that my past experience in office work as well as my training at the Baker Secretarial Academy have prepared me well. I would enjoy putting my skills to work in an office as exciting and as busy as yours.

If I am selected for the position, I will do my best to fill it well. Thank you again for your kindness.

Sincerely,

Evelyn Vickers

Evelyn Vickers

EV

A Choose a word or phrase about the letter on page 66 to answer the following questions.

1. What is Francine Summers's job?

   _____

2. Where does she work?

   _____

3. Why did Ms. Summers interview Evelyn Vickers?

   _____

4. Is the letter to Ms. Summers written in semiblock, block, or full block style?

   _____

5. What is the ZIP code of Salisbury, North Carolina?

   _____

6. What closing does Evelyn Vickers use?

   _____

7. Suggest three other closings that would be appropriate. Use necessary punctuation and capital letters.

   _____

   _____

   _____

8. Explain why the second version of the letter makes a better impression.

   _____

   _____

   _____

B Write a follow-up letter in block style that covers the following circumstances: a conference concerning the sender's promotion to second-shift production supervisor; Darrell G. Latour, Jr., General Manager; Thayer Construction Company, Inc.; 4467 Mount Union Street; Kent, Oklahoma 74103; September 15, 1999. Use your own name and address as sender. Abbreviate words that can be easily shortened.

Letters of Inquiry

Another common business letter is the letter of inquiry, or request. People write these letters to ask for information and services, such as free carpet samples, instructions on how to display the flag, estimates for upholstery cleaning, a map of a weekend campground, or a catalog of paperback books and videotapes for children. Like all business letters, the request follows a form. It is
- straightforward
- factual
- complete with names and dates
- specific about locations, catalog numbers, quantity, style, color, prices, and other facts about the exact product, information, or service requested
- explicit about where the requested material is to be sent

Other details that may be helpful are method of transportation (such as parcel post, UPS, overnight mail, or special delivery) and method of payment (such as cash, check, credit card, or money order). Study the sample letter that follows.

701 Dupont Lane
Lisbon, Ohio 44432
May 3, 1999

Dr. Marvin Bartels, Museum Director
Midwest Native American Culture Center
480 Seneca Avenue
Wichita, Kansas 67203

Dear Dr. Bartels:

I would be interested in receiving a brochure that includes dates and ticket prices for the upcoming exhibit of early Native American pottery.

Any information you could send me with regard to this exhibit would be greatly appreciated. I have enclosed a self-addressed stamped envelope. Thank you very much.

Sincerely,

Coleman Banks

Coleman Banks

CB/encl.

A Read the following incomplete request letter. Complete each blank
with an item from the list below.

Apt.   encl.   Association   February   SW
Gratefully yours Drive   Ohio   83   postage

Granville Plaza NE, **(a)** _____ 2

Greenville, **(b)** _____ 45331

(c) _____ 28, 1999

Manager
American Automobile **(d)** _____

(e) _____ Westchester **(f)** _____

Lima, Ohio 46806

Dear Sir:

    I am a member of AAA and am planning a trip by private van to San
Diego, California, in the next four weeks. This trip will include adults as well as
young children. I need information about sight-seeing, dining, and motels to
fit a modest budget.

    Please send a map, tour information, and guidebook about southern
California to the above address. I have enclosed $1.00 to pay for

(g) _____ .

                    (h) _____ ,

                    Samuel Walsh

                    Samuel Walsh

(i) _____ / **(j)** _____

B On the next page, write a letter of inquiry to a state agency that
arranges summer camps for physically challenged children. Make up
an address as well as the name of the agent. Ask for specific
instructions on selecting a camp for a ten-year-old child with asthma.
Mention that you can spend only $1,200 for the full two weeks.
Include an envelope for your inquiry.

_____

_____

_____

_____

_____

_____

_____

_____:

_____

_____

_____

_____

_____

_____

_____

_____

_____

_____

The Order Letter

Placing an order by mail often requires the use of a letter, especially when the company that you order from does not provide an order blank or does not accept telephone orders. Like the order request letter, this type of business letter requires much attention to detail. The sender should list the following information:

➤ exact name of the product, for example, Golden Maple Syrup
➤ catalog number and page, for instance, RE133 on p. 263
➤ exact size, such as Size 7 AA or Medium With Extra Long Sleeves
➤ color and alternate, if requested, such as red/blue
➤ quantity, for example, 1-gallon can
➤ material, such as denim, birch wood, or calfskin
➤ other identifying information, for example, petite, tall, or monogrammed

In addition to product information, the sender must compute the total price of the order. Usually a mail order includes price of shipping and handling along with local sales tax.

After these facts are stated, the sender should indicate other details, for example:

➤ where the package is to be shipped
➤ to whom the package is to be sent
➤ method of payment, such as cash, check, credit card, or money order
➤ special instructions, such as gift wrapped or insured

When the sender has no name to put in the receiver's place, the words "Customer Service" are appropriate. Read the following order letter to answer the questions.

6185 Glenview Terrace
Ardoch, North Dakota 58213
April 18, 1999

Customer Service
Woodland Friends, Inc.
800 Industrial Park
Menlo, Washington 98661

Dear Sir or Madam:

I would like to order the pine birdhouse found on page 74 of your spring catalog. It is the Rustic Ranch, catalog #710-D. The price is $13.49. I am enclosing a personal check for $15.99 to cover the cost of the birdhouse plus shipping and handling. Please gift wrap my order and send it by parcel post to Mrs. Elsie Danvers, 1553 Weddington Lane Northwest, Ardoch, North Dakota 58213.

Thanks,

Juan Danvers

Juan Danvers

JAD/encl.

A Indicate whether each statement below is *True* or *False*. Write your answer in the blank.

_____ 1. Juan Danvers is not buying a birdhouse for himself.

_____ 2. The check for $15.99 includes $2.50 to cover shipping and handling.

_____ 3. Mrs. Elsie Danvers is in the same town as Woodland Friends, Inc.

_____ 4. Juan Danvers is paying for the birdhouse with a credit card.

_____ 5. Woodland Friends, Inc., is in Washington, D.C.

_____ 6. Customer Service at Woodland Friends, Inc., charges extra if the catalog item is gift wrapped.

_____ 7. The sales tax on Juan Danvers's purchase is $2.50.

_____ 8. Juan Danvers wants the birdhouse to be shipped by parcel post.

_____ 9. Juan Danvers's middle name could be Andrew, but not Jeffrey.

_____ 10. Mrs. Elsie Danvers lives in the same town as Juan Danvers.

B On a separate sheet of paper, compose a block style letter from Jenny Whitcomb, Woodland Friends customer service representative, to Juan Danvers. Explain that your company must delay shipment of the Rustic Ranch birdhouse for at least two weeks unless the buyer is willing to take the birch model. Give the exact date when the pine birdhouse can be shipped and how it will be transported. Leave a telephone number that Juan Danvers may use to accept or reject Ms. Whitcomb's offer. Use "800" as the area code of the telephone number and explain that there is no charge for using the toll-free number.

C Read this advertisement for hot-air balloon rides. Then compose a letter to the company in which you make an appointment for a Saturday ride. Write your letter on the next page.

SATURDAY AND SUNDAY ONLY
MARCO'S MAGNIFICENT BALLOONS

Thrill to a morning launch over the beautiful mountains of Utah.

Photograph familiar landmarks as you float through clean air.
Have the time of your life—ride in style.
Select any one of Marco's four colorful hot-air balloons.
Relax in safety. Enjoy the ride.
Marco has been taking to the air for 25 years.
His satisfied customers can attest that he's the best.
Make your appointment now!
30 minutes, $75
Family Rates, 4 people, $275
Write to Marco, Box 81, Bluebell, Utah 84013

_____

_____

_____

_____

_____

_____

_____

_____:

_____

_____

_____

_____

_____

_____

_____

_____

_____

Sometimes the goods and services you receive are not acceptable. When you get a dress that is the wrong size, a mismatched set of towels, or a library reserve slip for an incorrect title, contact the business or agency immediately. If possible, photocopy the information you received to ensure clear, accurate communication. Enclose a business letter stating why the ordered merchandise or service does not meet your needs or expectations.

The concluding information in the letter explains to the company what action you expect them to take on the matter. State exactly what the company must do to make matters right. For example:
➤ refund
➤ replacement of goods
➤ credit slip
➤ other adjustment

Remember that emotions have no place in a business letter. No matter how annoyed or inconvenienced you may feel, keep a pleasant but firm tone throughout your letter. Consider these:

> I don't think your company does a very good job of mailing boxes to customers.

> The box you mailed to me was crushed on one corner by the time I received it.

Notice that the second example describes the unacceptable box without placing blame for the damage. The writer of the second sentence, by remaining unemotional, is more likely to receive a positive reaction from the company. The first writer mistakenly puts the company on the defensive by making a broad accusation. Most reputable companies quickly and gladly correct errors, so it is not necessary to accuse or be negative.

To make sure that your complaint letter will be effective, send it to a specific person if possible. If you don't know the receiver's name, address your remarks to Customer Service. Follow this model:

> Customer Service
> International Exchange
> 19 Grover Avenue
> Green River, Wyoming 82935

Complaints sometimes require more than one communication before the problem is resolved. There are several things that you can do to assure that you will get satisfaction. For example:
➤ Keep a copy of your correspondence.
➤ Circle on the calendar the date you sent the letter.
➤ Be prepared to supply all information about the transaction.
➤ Explain what letters have passed between you and the company or agency and to whom they were written.
➤ Don't give up until you have done everything possible to reach a settlement of the difficulty.

One Edwards Place
Columbia, South Carolina 29261
March 7, 1999

Julian M. McGuin, President
Acme Pest Control
10007 Highland Boulevard
Columbia, South Carolina 29263

Dear Mr. McGuin:
      When your serviceman came to my house around 3:00 P.M. Thursday,
March 4, to remove a swarm of bees, he drove over the curb. His truck destroyed
a drain pipe and damaged a culvert.
      I expect Acme Pest Control to have this damage repaired immediately at
the company's expense. I will appreciate your assistance in clearing up this
unfortunate incident. I look forward to your reply.

                              Respectfully,

                              Ms. Renee Withers

                              Ms. Renee Withers

RW

A Study the model above to answer the following questions.

1. Who is making the complaint?

_____

2. What closing does the sender use?

_____

3. Suggest three other appropriate closings for a letter of complaint. Use necessary punctuation
   and capital letters.

   a. _____

   b. _____

   c. _____

4. To whom is the complaint addressed?

_____

5. When did the damage occur?

_____

6. Whom does the sender blame?

_____

7. Whom does the sender expect to pay for repairs?

_____

8. What two objects must be replaced or repaired?

_____

9. In what state did the incident take place?

_____

10. Why was the company called?

_____

B On the next page, compose a semiblock letter from Julian McGuin, President of Acme Pest Control, dated March 9, to Ms. Renee Withers. Agree to Ms. Withers's demands for repairs to her yard. Name the company that will do the work. State the date and time when the repairs will be completed. Indicate with your initials that you typed Julian McGuin's reply.

_____

_____

_____

_____

_____

_____

_____

_____:

_____

_____

_____

_____

_____

_____

_____

_____

_____

Sometimes you may need to write a letter to a foreign country. For example, you may have a pen pal, relative, or friend who lives in another country. Also, you might wish to order something from a foreign company. Business and friendly letters that are sent to foreign countries often contain unusual elements in the address. When writing to any address outside the United States, follow exactly the necessary information. State your return address as usual, but end with "USA." Consider this model:

> Rep. Stan Jessup, Jr.
> 18 Del Toro Way
> Questa, New Mexico 87556 USA

A Complete the following envelope with information from the model return address above. Draw a stamp where it should go.

Shinglee Publishers
120 Hillview Ave.
#05-06/07
Kewalram Hillview
Singapore 2355

ATTN: LOH MUN WAI

B Compose a list of five activities you might want to describe to a foreign pen pal.

1. _____

2. _____

3. _____

4. _____

5. _____

C Make a similar list of five questions you could ask about activities in a foreign country.

1. _____

2. _____

3. _____

4. _____

5. _____

D Using some of the items on your two lists, compose a letter to a pen pal in a distant land. Write your letter on a separate sheet of paper.

E Using the information below about a sender, address an envelope to yourself. Abbreviate where appropriate.

B & B School Supplies
450 Matheson Boulevard East
Unit 58
Ottawa, Ontario K2P OB6 Canada

Review Unit 2—Part 1

Use this section of your workbook to review the concepts that were introduced in lessons one through eleven in your Business Letters unit. This will give you many opportunities to practice analyzing and writing business letters.

Parts of a Business Letter

A Read the letter below. Identify the lettered parts. If you have any questions, refer to page 36.

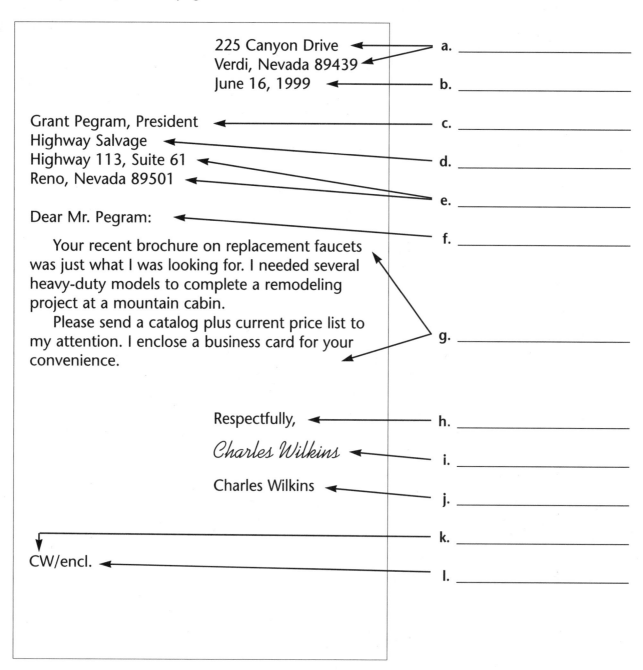

225 Canyon Drive   a. _____
Verdi, Nevada 89439
June 16, 1999   b. _____

Grant Pegram, President   c. _____
Highway Salvage
Highway 113, Suite 61   d. _____
Reno, Nevada 89501

    e. _____

Dear Mr. Pegram:

    f. _____

Your recent brochure on replacement faucets was just what I was looking for. I needed several heavy-duty models to complete a remodeling project at a mountain cabin.

Please send a catalog plus current price list to my attention. I enclose a business card for your convenience.   g. _____

Respectfully,   h. _____

Charles Wilkins   i. _____

Charles Wilkins   j. _____

    k. _____

CW/encl.   l. _____

The Three Types of a Business Letter

B Answer *Yes* or *No* to the following questions about semiblock, block, and full block letter style.

Semiblock

_____ 1. Is the sender's address placed at the left margin?

_____ 2. Is the first line of the body indented?

_____ 3. Is the greeting followed by a colon?

_____ 4. Does it include the receiver's name and address?

_____ 5. Is the closing followed by a comma?

Block

_____ 1. Is the sender's address placed at the left margin?

_____ 2. Is the first line of the body indented?

_____ 3. Is the greeting followed by a colon?

_____ 4. Does it include the receiver's name and address?

_____ 5. Is the closing followed by a comma?

Full Block

_____ 1. Is the sender's address placed at the left margin?

_____ 2. Is the first line of the body indented?

_____ 3. Is the greeting followed by a colon?

_____ 4. Does it include the receiver's name and address?

_____ 5. Is the closing followed by a comma?

Greetings, Closings, and Addresses

C Place an X by each example of a greeting, closing, or address below that is complete and appropriate for business letters.

Greetings

_____ 1. Hi Mattie!
_____ 2. Dear Professor Greeley:
_____ 3. Dear Randall,
_____ 4. Gentlemen,

Closings

_____ 5. See you later,
_____ 6. Affectionately,
_____ 7. With sincere regards,
_____ 8. Respectfully,

Addresses

_____ 9. Ms. Yvonne Stone, Director
Central Warehouse
11 Parkway Circle
Warner, New Hampshire 03278

_____ 11. Mrs. Delia Thayer, Reference
Librarian
Riley Library
96 Main Avenue
Riley, Kansas 66531

_____ 10. Dr. J. S. Shepherd
Surgical Center
Rittergasse 9
4051 Basel
Switzerland

_____ 12. Bob Liu, Product Manager
Roadside Express
89-C Denton Complex
Mount Holly, North Carolina

Letters of Apology

D Below are several choices of opening sentences from letters of apology. Select the one in each group that seems most appropriate. On the lines that follow, give reasons for your choice.

1. **a.** I guess you know why I'm writing this letter, Mrs. Damian.

   b. The accident in the dining room was my stupid fault.

   c. I am so sorry about the spill on the dining room carpet during last week's lunch meeting.

   _____

   _____

   _____

2. **a.** We regret that our dog damaged the rose bed outside your hotel Wednesday afternoon.

   b. Fluffy sends her apologies.

   c. In case you haven't noticed, one of your rosebushes is missing.

   _____

   _____

   _____

3. **a.** Several of your neighbors told me that I should explain the dented mailbox.

   b. I am sorry that my truck banged into your mailbox last Thursday morning.

   c. The accident at the mailbox was my fault.

   _____

   _____

   _____

4. a. In opening my mail this morning, I accidentally ripped open a letter that belonged to you.

   b. The mailman put your letter in my box again, and I ripped it open without reading the address.

   c. Your letter got ripped by mistake. I'm sorry.

_____

_____

_____

How to Place an Order

E Using the information below, complete an order letter for one of the products. Supply a company address. First write a draft of your letter below.

1. State flags, either 4" x 6" or 7" x 8 1/2", mounted on maple or pine sticks. Flags can be ordered in cotton or silk for each of the fifty states, Guam, and the Virgin Islands. Prices are as follows: 1–5 flags, $4.98 each; 6–10 flags, $4.50 each; 11 or more flags, $4.25 each. Shipping is included in the purchase price.

2. Winter skin ointment to prevent and heal chapped lips and hands. One 6-ounce tube sells for $3.47. A 12-ounce tube sells for $6.98. Shipping is $1.25 for regular mail or $3.25 for express delivery. Orders mailed by the end of this month receive a free guide to U.S. ski resorts.

3. A four-compartment fireproof computer-disk container costs $32.95. It comes in high-impact plastic. Choose from gray, black, red, or green. Add 7% for postage and handling. If you prefer the more compact three-compartment container, the price is only $28.95.

4. Camouflage tape costs 17 cents per yard up to 15 yards. Bulk rolls sell for the following prices: 15 yards—$2.10; 30 yards—$4.00; 60 yards—$7.25. Be sure to include $2.25 for postage and handling. Choose from basic brown or green. For extra protection in the wild, enclose 50 cents for a 10-yard sample of our orange reflective tape.

_____

_____

_____

_____

_____

_____

_____

How to Write a Letter of Instruction

F Using the information below, complete a letter of instruction for one of the following situations. Supply addresses. First write a draft of your letter below.

1. Discuss with a friend the best way to put up, take down, and store a tent. Include information about location, layout, and protection from bad weather.

2. Describe how to make a banner for a holiday. Stress a variety of artistic supplies, messages, and the approximate size for maximum attention.

3. Explain how to hem a pair of jeans. Give an accurate description of how to mark the right length, how to allow for shrinkage, and how to cut off excess material before making the final seam.

4. Describe how to train a dog to fetch. Begin with puppy training. Name a few objects that puppies like to play with. Then explain how to get the dog to find them and bring them back.

5. Discuss the best way to display a house number. Suggest how to fasten the number on the house and where the number might be most easily seen. Emphasize several reasons why homeowners would want their house numbers visible during the day and the night.

Letter to the Editor

G Look through several newspapers for two letters that take opposite positions on a particular issue. With a partner, orally summarize the point of view of each letter. Then answer the following questions about each.

First Letter	**Second Letter**
1. At what point in the letter does the writer state an opinion: beginning, middle, or end?	1. At what point in the letter does the writer state an opinion: beginning, middle, or end?
2. What aspect of the topic does the writer stress?	2. What aspect of the topic does the writer stress?
3. Does the letter display emotion? How?	3. Does the letter display emotion? How?
4. Does the writer give examples to prove a point? Name several.	4. Does the writer give examples to prove a point? Name several.
5. Does the writer conclude with a convincing argument? Explain.	5. Does the writer conclude with a convincing argument? Explain.

H Explain in a few sentences which letter conforms to your own way of thinking and why.

I On a separate sheet of paper, write your own letter to the editor on the same subject. State your opinion clearly and unemotionally. Give original reasons for your opinion. Conclude with a strong statement of belief.

Review Unit 2—Part 2

Letters of Application

A On a separate sheet of paper, write a letter of application to McNalley's Old-Fashioned Dime Store. Stress information from the résumé on page 64 that would indicate your qualifications for the job of cashier. When you have finished the first draft of your letter, answer the following questions about the finished product.

_____ 1. Have I named the specific job that I am applying for?

_____ 2. Have I given reasons why I am suited to that job?

_____ 3. Have I discussed my educational and job record?

_____ 4. Have I given clear information about myself and where I can be reached?

_____ 5. Have I presented myself as positively as I can?

The Job Advertisement

B Select one of the job advertisements below. Compose a résumé and job application for the position. Then, on a separate sheet of paper, compose a follow-up letter after your first interview.

1. WANTED: Trainee for warehouse clerk. Applicant should be eager for advancement and willing to learn. Contact Wm. Steele, Gen Mgr., after 2 Wed. or Fri. (776) 555-0011. EOE.

2. Needed immediately—sitter for aged parent. Light lifting and meal preparation req. Send résumé and refs. to Georgia Granger, 8718 Cumberland Terrace, Forest, Ohio 45843.

3. Need office asst. for wood products lab. Must be at least 16. Call (993) 555-4149 9:00–5:00 Mon.–Sat. Ask for Pers. Mgr. or lv. msg. with sec.

Ad Abbreviations

C Write the letter of the word or phrase that shows what each abbreviation means.

a. secretary   **c.** leave message   **e.** assistant
b. references   **d.** required   **f.** Equal Opportunity Employer

_____ 1. req.   _____ 3. ref.   _____ 5. EOE

_____ 2. asst.   _____ 4. lv. msg.   _____ 6. sec.

Abbreviations

D Write the abbreviation for each word that follows.

1. Senator _____
2. assistant _____
3. references _____
4. President _____
5. secretary _____

6. required _____
7. Captain _____
8. Reverend _____
9. Drive _____
10. General _____

Greetings and Closings

E Write three examples of greetings and closings that would be used in a business letter. Be sure to punctuate them correctly.

Greetings	**Closings**
1. _____	4. _____
2. _____	5. _____
3. _____	6. _____

Now contrast these by writing three examples of greetings and closings that would be used in a friendly letter. Be sure to punctuate them correctly.

Greetings	**Closings**
7. _____	10. _____
8. _____	11. _____
9. _____	12. _____

Résumés

F Put an X in front of each piece of information that would be found in a résumé.

_____ 1. references
_____ 2. educational experience
_____ 3. telephone number
_____ 4. age and sex

_____ 5. work history
_____ 6. race
_____ 7. outside interests
_____ 8. number of children

REVIEW

Letter Styles

G Write *Yes* or *No* under each heading to answer each question.

Semiblock   **Block**   **Full Block**

_____   _____   _____   1. Is the sender's address placed at the left margin?

_____   _____   _____   2. Is the greeting of the letter followed by a colon?

_____   _____   _____   3. Is each of the paragraphs in the letter indented?

_____   _____   _____   4. Are the receiver's name and address included in the inside address?

_____   _____   _____   5. Does the closing begin at the left margin?

Letter of Complaint

H On a separate sheet of paper, compose a letter of complaint to the Scare You Company, a business that sells party supplies. Mr. Donald Holly is the head of Customer Service. Scare You is located at 317 Orchard Avenue in New York, New York 10010. Explain that the shipment of silver-wedding anniversary decorations arrived too late for you to use. Suggest a way for the company to satisfy you, perhaps by sending a truck to pick up the merchandise or offering a refund.

Business Envelope

I Create an envelope to accompany the letter you wrote above.

1. _____

2. _____

3. _____

4. _____

5. _____

6. _____

7. _____

End-of-Book Test

Types of Letters

A Write F if the type of letter named is an example of a friendly letter. Write B if it is an example of a business letter.

_____ 1. formal invitation   _____ 6. complaint

_____ 2. application   _____ 7. postcard

_____ 3. congratulations   _____ 8. thank you

_____ 4. to the editor   _____ 9. apology

_____ 5. instruction   _____ 10. informal invitation

Style of Letter

B Write each word or phrase under the heading where it belongs. You will write some words or phrases under both headings.

closing followed by a comma   colon after greeting   address of sender
address of receiver   date   comma after greeting
title after receiver's name   informal tone

Friendly Letter

1. _____
2. _____
3. _____
4. _____
5. _____

Business Letter

6. _____
7. _____
8. _____
9. _____
10. _____

Postal Codes and Abbreviations

C Write the word or phrase that tells what each set of letters means.

_____ 1. Rd.   _____ 7. Ave.

_____ 2. TX   _____ 8. OR

_____ 3. Gen.   _____ 9. refs.

_____ 4. asst.   _____ 10. dept.

_____ 5. encl.   _____ 11. IA

_____ 6. AL   _____ 12. Sec.

Letter Facts

D Mark the following statements about letters *True* or *False.*

_____ 1. Invitations should tell the occasion, event, place, time, and date.

_____ 2. A friendly letter has a greeting that is followed by a colon.

_____ 3. A sympathy note includes statements concerning your emotional response to someone's loss.

_____ 4. An envelope for a business letter includes the name of the company of the receiver.

_____ 5. A block style business letter has indented paragraphs.

_____ 6. The letters ATTN are found at the end of a friendly letter.

_____ 7. The inside address includes a person's title.

_____ 8. In a résumé, a listing of work history is not important.

_____ 9. The closing "Love" should not be used in a friendly letter.

_____ 10. In the full block style of a business letter, all lines begin at the left.

Envelopes

E Use your name in the upper left-hand corner for the return address.
Use the information that follows to complete the envelope.

| Kaysville | Customer Service | 84037 | Ms. | UT |
| Schmidt | Lakeview Road | 217 | Diane | Five Star Music Company |

1. _____

2. _____

3. _____

                                        4. _____

                                        5. _____

                                        6. _____

                                        7. _____

Glossary

Aligned placed in a line, one under the other

Block style similar to the semiblock style, this style of business letter does not indent each paragraph of the body. To show the change from one paragraph to another, the writer must skip one line.

Body the central part of a letter where the writer states facts and asks questions of the receiver

Brochure pamphlet or booklet

cc the abbreviation for *carbon copy.* The abbreviation is used at the end of a business letter to show who has received copies of the letter.

Closing the final remark from the writer, indicating that the message of the letter is ended

Controversial causing disagreement

Correspondence letters and other forms of communication

Credit slip a receipt that can be exchanged for goods

Customer service a worker or department that solves customer disputes concerning quality of goods or services

E-mail short for *electronic mail.* Messages are sent from one person to another by E-mail by using computers.

Enclosed included in an envelope with a letter

Engraved a shape forced onto paper by a heavy stamp

FAX short for *facsimile;* a machine similar to a photocopier that transmits documents and pictures over long distances by using telephone lines

Full block style a way of arranging a business letter in which all information is aligned at the left-hand margin. Like the block style letter, the writer must skip a line between paragraphs in the body.

Greeting the part of a letter that speaks directly to the receiver

Heading	the sender's address followed by the date
Inquiry	a request for information
Inside address	in a business letter, the receiver's address
Internet	a complex network of computers that are linked together
Modem	a machine that sends written communications from a computer over a telephone
Money order	a receipt for money that is sent through the mail in the place of cash or a check
Point of view	the attitude and manner by which a person thinks about something
Postal card	same as a postcard
Postal code	two capital letters without punctuation identifying a particular state
Postcard	a small card that provides space for a brief message that can be sent through the mail. It often contains a picture
Reference	the name of a person who can testify to a person's honesty, skill, or character
Reference initials	initials of the letter writer alongside the initials of the typist
Reimburse	pay back
Résumé	a complete list of jobs, education, and experiences during a person's career
R.S.V.P.	the French phrase *"Répondez, s'il vous plaît,"* meaning "Please reply"
Semiblock style	a way of arranging information for a business letter in which the sender's address, the closing, and the signature are toward the right-hand margin, the receiver's address borders the left-hand margin, and each paragraph of the body is indented

Signature   the author's name in his or her own handwriting

TELEX   a method of communicating using typewriters connected by telegraph wires

Toll free   without charge or fee

Tone   the author's attitude, indicated by the kind of words he or she chooses. A tone can be formal or informal.

UPS   United Parcel Service; the largest package delivery service in the United States

World Wide Web the name for a complex group of linked computers; sometimes called the Internet

ZIP code   a number code developed by the Post Office for sorting mail more quickly and easily (ZIP stands for Zone Improvement Plan)

KEY TO POSTAL ABBREVIATIONS FOR STATES

Alabama	**AL**	Montana	**MT**
Alaska	**AK**	Nebraska	**NE**
Arizona	**AZ**	Nevada	**NV**
Arkansas	**AR**	New Hampshire	**NH**
California	**CA**	New Jersey	**NJ**
Colorado	**CO**	New Mexico	**NM**
Connecticut	**CT**	New York	**NY**
District of Columbia	**DC**	North Carolina	**NC**
Delaware	**DE**	North Dakota	**ND**
Florida	**FL**	Ohio	**OH**
Georgia	**GA**	Oklahoma	**OK**
Hawaii	**HI**	Oregon	**OR**
Idaho	**ID**	Pennsylvania	**PA**
Illinois	**IL**	Rhode Island	**RI**
Indiana	**IN**	South Carolina	**SC**
Iowa	**IA**	South Dakota	**SD**
Kansas	**KS**	Tennessee	**TN**
Kentucky	**KY**	Texas	**TX**
Louisiana	**LA**	Utah	**UT**
Maine	**ME**	Vermont	**VT**
Maryland	**MD**	Virginia	**VA**
Massachusetts	**MA**	Washington	**WA**
Michigan	**MI**	West Virginia	**WV**
Minnesota	**MN**	Wisconsin	**WI**
Mississippi	**MS**	Wyoming	**WY**
Missouri	**MO**		